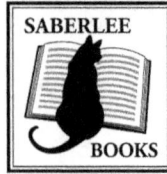

Published by

Saberlee Books
Los Angeles, CA
saberleebooks@yahoo.com
Published February 2013

Editor: Lisette Brodey/www.lisettebrodey.com
Copy Editor: Laura Daly/laurajdaly@earthlink.net
Cover Design: Charles Roth/cmrdesignca@gmail.com
Cover Photos: Lisette Brodey
Author Photo: Lisette Brodey

Book is set in Minion Pro (12/14.4)
Titles set in Lucida Handwriting

ISBN-13: 978-0-9815836-0-0 (paperback)
ISBN-10: 0-9815836-0-1

ISBN-13: 978-0-9815836-7-9 (e-book)
0-9815836-7-9

Poetry

Printed in the United States of America

To my children, Lisette and Kenneth

"I'm proud of you and of these."

Ellen Coyne Masters, wife of Edgar Lee Masters

Acknowledgments

Heartfelt thanks to those who helped to make this book a reality: Laura Daly, Leatrice Gant, Lisa McCallum, Charles Roth, and Laura Schultz.

TABLE OF CONTENTS

ON THE PERSISTENCE OF MEMORY

MY WAY TO ANYWHERE

THE MUSE

FRIENDSHIP

My Way to Anywhere

Jean Lisette Brodey

Edited by:
Lisette Brodey

On the Persistence of Memory

ON THE PERSISTENCE OF MEMORY

Sky is static
Water may be dead
though no one can be sure
It still reflects.

Time is draped
over a tree
and there is soul or image of soul
lying in limbo

Memory is image
spewing larvae
until numbers vanish and beetles clog
the face of time.

TELEMACHUS AND THE EIGHTH STREET DINER

I get so goddamned tired of the same faces night after night
      That woman makes her choice with fanatical precision
      deciding on dinner
      with defiance in her voice,
as if indecision
(roast pork or chicken) could erase
Dear Sir, your letter of the eighth received.

We said goodbye in a cloak room.
What a fantastic place for a benediction,
      There sitting in the last booth,
      she must be over eighty,
      past caring now
      for anything but show;
      refusing to admit
      that the tea is spilt
      and the toast cold with midnight hours away.

On the weekends there are parties
but I prefer my trivia unadorned.
      Waiting at the counter,
      shadow in her eyes, looking
      toward the mirror
      with an unwieldy stare—
      consistency is sudden
      down to the silver buttons.
      Truth has hung by less than dark roots of hair.

Oh, Mother, do not taunt me with disguise
for I am weary with the weight of dreams
and cursed with having known—
return unto me.

TURTLELIKE HE LAY WRITHING

Turtlelike he lay writhing,
like a turtle unshelling—

only she
could catch
the motion of his agony;

only she
could watch elated at
the anguish of his turns.

Then
in one great gesture
he passed
the fine talent of his shell.

Useless
it lay in the hard gray cove
and she moved
beyond remembrance.

OF AN UNFINISHED STATUE

She calls it Wedlock,
the wet clay of her mornings
draped in a privacy of incompletion.
Visitors shuffle as the cover falls
Eyeless ovals
stare from a single slab
of breast or stocks or guillotine that
shatters with a broken blade. Notice
the head on the left
        has a bit more clay.

TRIPTYCH

Abstraction vaunted
still abstraction
though horses of memory
bring forth shod.

Minds evoke
new ranches from
drying hides—love
from quarried gestures.

Demands break
according to time
or weather forgetting
how hearts must beat.

ISLE AU HAUT

Waves break where men
with faces of their dead kneel
as prophets in the palm of a God.
They walk to the beat of water
and die to the knell of sea.

Summer people
fill the gull wind with shouts
and dabble in communion. Forgotten
fish lie rotting on the dock
while weavers mend their nets.

  Ralph Weaver built a wooden fence
around the family stones last summer
    when the lobster run was slow
                Josiah
          father of Abigail
            Martha
         mother of Paul
           Herbert
drown'd at Whitehead Pt., Penobscot Bay
       February 24, 1844
    16 years, 2 months and 20 days.

STRANGERS (For Albert Camus)

We sit around a broad pine-wood table
discussing metaphysics. Across
the road magnolias bloom
on the ground of the
HOME FOR THE BLIND.

In an hour the train arrives in Newark.
That woman by the aisle forgot her
ticket. The conductor stares.
She reminds him of
his dead sister.

The new widow tries on a yellow dress
she saw it in the store window.
Her husband's older brother
and his wife are coming
for dinner.

My young son, visiting great-aunt Maria
in the nursing home, amuses himself
waving to reflections. She
talks about childhood and
recites nursery rhymes.

Is there anything to say to a mother
whose only son has died? I think
I will take her some apple cake.
The poet saw loneliness
in falling leaves.

CAMUS

Surveyors and statisticians
Block off the world in empty squares:
Sentries log the twilight tides
And restless pace of dunes,
Allowing extra
For rain clouds, trying thus to learn
The width and breadth of a vigil
And density of a dream.
Needles quiver, instruments break,
Men are called away
with propositions still unsolved
While the watch goes on by the sea.

Once a divinity was drawn
To create roses and to make
For the prodigal eternal feast,
His glory was chanted
Through the chain of years.
At last the choristers grew
Tired of echoing psalms
And laid the cornerstone for
A temple of ultimate time.
But a maze grew round.
The way to the site was set
And thorns by the path dug deep.

Where is the path for those who
Live in empty squares and seek
Meaning in the horizon?
A stranger of sun's domain,

Knowing the landmarks,
Plotted a course for those who
Travel unaccompanied
Across the deserted beach.
He planned a caravan,
Its destination
Was to be the meridian
Its route was across the earth.

A streak of shining steel forged
With impatience of the age
Crashed. The stranger too was called
Before his charts were drawn.
Will there be draftsmen
To draw from his lines and guides
To follow his desert route?
Will there be archers to their bows
Beneath a new sun?
Are there rebels to go forth?
We mourn him: therefore they exist.

LINES TO BE INSCRIBED ON A COFFIN

Ha! Here's the proper pad
for my profundities—
a stranger's box.
Here lies the total sum
of his unveilings
and my creative paradox.
I compose with mordant passion
as boys scrawl on toilet doors.
His bones reacted much the same
and carved a coffin—nothing more.
Our motives mock us in their lust.
Lines and bones must turn to dust.

ELIZABETH:
THE HOUSEWIFE AS A YOUNG ROBOT

Betsy is busy spilling children
over Eldritch Park—
the fecund cradle,
changeling of her brain.
She passed from thought
lo many years ago,
and now at thirty-eight
she stands stripped to the womb
with vacant hands enmeshed
in the sound of gavels SALE
diapers pudding teas.
She stares in rapt disinterest
at a series of aprons
projects and cats.
Betsy is busy spilling
        all over Eldritch Park.

DESTINATION

In the sun swarming months of spring he wandered
With the wind brushed core of his being
Diffused thru the promise of clad air.
In his turn, a sponge for the season's life,
He absorbed of the bud filled earth,
A fragment in the eternal design.

Now on he strode thru the green warmth
Of all the earth throbbing days
And planted his seed in summer's womb.
With the acorn and the jewel weed
It flourished to vibrancy
Becoming a cell in the vernal flow.

In his orchard hours,
He gave of his reddened apples
To nourish those who walked among the trees
Into all the corners of time.
Then in his white moment, he quickened
And sought the turn in the infinite road.

His quest led him thru a maze of rootless
        bushes.
Bowed low with gaudy dreams.
Chasing gossamer clad phantoms of his August
        afternoons
thru the shadowy garden, he fell exhausted.
Never knowing that he slept.
'Neath boughs of living fruit.

CREDO

Weathered houses of men
Whirl in the heightening flood, whirl
In the waters of spring
While gnawing memories of men
See still a soft summer flow
Giving growth to land of its shores.

Desolate stalks of wheat
Twist in the sand-brown loam, die
In the scorch of noon
In the scornful rays of the sun
That warmed through the vernal womb
Once bursting with hopeful grain.

Who will worship a god
That knows not his handiwork?
What peace to those who plod
From the firm guardian of tides,
Who cares not for trivial poles
As he shapes a trembling globe? Then

I will praise graven gods
Molded of humble clay that
Cry out from their temples
For frail offerings of drifted love
And though these gods pass and change
I will worship them through the winding
        of all my days.

My Way to Anywhere

WORDS

Because I choose it thus,
the ride leads
a pleasant woodland way:
summer fullness,
leaf sky—
lights too small
for scanning,
the bent place
where a stream
makes its running
felt. I brake
to acknowledge a blossom.

And the river
still as a dream
reflects trees
doubling
ending
in themselves.
Into the car's path
a pheasant, on a bush
a singing bird.
The day denies
a need for dream
because I choose it thus.

THURSDAYS DEMAND EXISTENCE

I dreamed
her dead and dwell
on dreams with guilt
that burns in
every outlet.
Days would name
this half-sought sin
but my pen
lies buried under
bells and scrapings
of a dozen
stupid cans,
beneath
dumb groceries
in a world
where Thursday
demands existence.
Clocks tick
on every nerve
and children
are a million alleys
filled with
calling cats.
Pictures
are crooked
and I clutch
an empty pad.

CONTEMPORARY

son of adam's first dog
sitting on porcelain haunches
begone—
and take that grecian mirror!

this time demands a subtler clutter—
buddhas with ivory navels
and fish
with wooden walleyes

dog of the rainbow, stay
in the attic with daffodils
a curse on all your heirlooms.

TANA (N) AGER IS SPLELLED WORONG

Here sits my red bird of a muse perched on a dropping bough;
From spirals of ecstatic flight she rests exhausted now.
Only for you she sounded her precious avian trill.
It was your Philistine soul her spirit sought to fill
By bringing poetry's magic to your superbly mundane earth.
Really, Val, at a time like this, what is one word's worth?

PORTRAIT

Face writ with the totality of her every hour,
Eyes that echo with the rhythm of epic breath,
Strength of smile mesmerizing with a vital power,
These the vibrant similes of poetic depth.
The lustrous dignity of her quintessence
Lies beneath a manifest meter of patterned days,
While flouting reticence of her soul's true essence
    Reserves for few, heart chosen, the secret of the phrase.
Living promise of the past unfolds
Creating her present's vibrant rhyme.
Each stanza of fullest being holds
A key for those in the midst of time.
No myth drawn muse for midwife of my quilled art's birth
She will be my sonnet, my poem's throbbing worth.

RECIPIENT

Aristotle said
that poetry implies
either
a special gift of nature
or a strain of madness

I would
incline toward the latter view—
it takes a bit of madness to spin
rocks around in search of newts
when woods are towering with pine.

Then, too,
there are certain ecstasies
that sanity could never stand
excoriations that excite
madmen to their paeans
Reason
could never wait summer-struck
or watch night skies without
swatting insects—only lunatics
and poets can ignore gnats.

Here among the hedgerow
I reread the Grecian lines
and mark the margin
with minor corrections
for the century.

Poetry implies
a strain of madness,
the special gift of nature.

The Muse

LIZALEE

Lizalee
carries two potatoes in a red
      leather pocketbook,
contemplates the world
      through knotholes—
seeks comfort in catnip
      and a fear of hats,
brushes her teeth before
      supper, fine points
all guaranteed to assure
      a spanking commotion.
While deploring the look of
      her own brute face,
she scrubs the mirrors clean.
      Lizalee,
like a catamount, maintains
      a hold on the human race—
      the precipice edge
        with fingertips.

VAGUE CANDLES

Vague candles
With shadow light
Brush the mirror hall
Where costumed revelers whirl in patterned dance.
Here my
Veiless cadence
Glides unseen
For masks will finely blind as they conceal.

Across the parquetry
An ivory duchess
Vacuity adorned
Pauses to regard my open step.
Then fearfully
She strikes the
Paltry chord
To which her whining courtiers are attuned.

A skulking guest
His shiny mask
No longer guise
Avoids the stinging tempo of my waltz.
This pallid spectator
Mingles softly
With reflections
That see as truth his colored satin lie.

My poet soul
Bows question
To the exquisite, those who

Unwrinkle this, their sudden suitor, in a taut stare.
Monotonously regretting,
They quiet my
Sundering rite
To await serene promise from a proper palm.

Then, clothed
In the reckless gown
Of your reality
You turn to me across the brittle hour
We listen to the
Uttering voice of
Our unguarded depths
No longer deafened by the pounding rhythm of the masquerade.

MUSE FOUND AMONG THE TEACUPS

I met her unexpectedly
While on my way to anywhere
And dropped my silly errand
When she asked me in for tea.

Next day I took another walk
To see her and to chat again
Our minutes strode right on to jar
The vagrant hours from the clock.

From those words on I had no heart
For corner cupboard memories
And everyday lay shattered there
Where tea-time talk turned into art.

She stole the wisps of meaning straight
From my small world of sometime ways
And left behind her tempest gift
My blessed power to create.

SKETCHES FOR A SELF-PORTRAIT

I crush a crawling ant
On the sundial base in emulation of time
As waspish minutes snap at my afternoon
Soon there will be more ants and more minutes
Until it all becomes encased in shadow.

In alpine hours I seek
The highest places scorning languid valleys,
Discovering again at every climb
That crests can be tedious as coves
And always, the descent from scorn is hard.

When the wind blew me his name
I pulled it apart balancing the letters
Like thirteen silvery balls. Then the word fell.
No one who saw me stopped to applaud
Although I was the very best of jugglers.

I was shaped by Sorrow
That churlish sculptor who carves the living stone.
Though I chafe now and despise his art,
The chiseled scar of grief does not vanish.
A statue can never escape its knife.

Among the silent trees
There floats the muffled counsel of my words.
I would listen to its echoing chorus
But in the forest darkness I am afraid
And seek the choiring solace of other songs.

When I wear passion's cloak
I am enslaved whether love or justice rules.
Yet why be free to wear a weary gray?
Pity the simpering patrician—
I shall dress in saffron and bend my knee.

These misty ecstasies
On the capes of earth, mountain peaks
I love and fear are my epitome.
Yet their light is sensitive to the hours
Like a star that flares and falls and disappears.
Still I shall not seek substance
In eternal glades. Time has no destination
But silver moods have made the pilgrim's role.
The cosmos of their creation brings
Transcendence to the transience of my soul.

Friendship

HER WORDS

I brought my poems and she read
Catching the awkward rise of light.
"I'm proud of you—and of these," she said
Then we turned in our talk to greater heights
And my lines lay
        still in the passing night.
She had walked slowly in my stride.
I became poet in her pride.

I look from here to a past hour
And her gift. Was it accepted
In a bond of pride or spurned with anger?
Did love of solidness of silence met
Lead from that distant
        cantle of her years?
Perhaps, strong like a sovereign bird
She rose and flew beyond the word.

But most must soar on her waxen wings.
Caught by earth, they await the sky
That a lesser-day Daedalus can bring.
This is the metaphor of human lives
Yet love still quivers
        like an injured thing
And fear hides hearts from destiny
While pilgrims fall into the sea.

Words fly above wet fields with wind;
Words fly like seeds from autumn pods
To perish rootless on a weathered whin
Or to be borne to fruit in a fertile sod
Where the furrows
      of harvest are thin.
O, wind will spiral without heed
But soil lies fallow without seed.

ELEMENTS OF A FRIENDSHIP

Pulsating steel,
aglow on forge of our
igniting intimacy
is tempered by strains
from my unfleeing past.

Discordant sparks,
clinging quarrels
now wholly mine,
strain the temper in
our smoldering moment.

Brilliant diamond,
set in jealous time's
circling bond,
reflects prismatic change
from distant sun.

Discarded disk,
once whirling facets
from uncut stone,
changes my reflection
on your slender thrusts.

Mountain's stream,
tortuous gatherer
of bank and bed,
courses terrestrial growth
to sole fulfillment.

Consummate water,
mysterious receiver
of unsettled flow, now
grown through shifting course
to deepened tranquility.

CONSTANT AS LOVE

Dearest Friend,
     I would explain—

a quarrel and
you hasten to a symmetry
but my limb resists…
     Hemispheres disagree
on sunset and kaleidoscopes
turn on shattered glass.
Birth must be divergence.
     Do not prod
concordance nor conspire
against existing nights.
Give sanctuary to discontent
and let quarrel be constant as love.

FRIENDSHIP

friendship is an illusion, a nonexistent staff for
the unsteady traveler to lean upon.
It is but the grove at the crossroads where two paths
unite beneath the shade of a tree and then go on again.

friendship is
    A ball of snow, glistening, pure, and precious—the
circle melts from the heat of the palm.
    The wine, deep, royal, bidding in the goblet—the
ruby disappears as you sip.
    That moon, protecting, inspiring, and comforting—the
planet will go with the morning light.

A life without friendship is empty. The void of our days
must be filled with a wet palm, an empty goblet and a flaming
yellow ball that parches the verdant earth.

A PARALLELOGRAM AS SEEN FROM THE INSIDE

Phyllis was there.
Phyllis was always there
fastened to the bottom of days.

You and I walked through
nascent twilight,
snowy moon.
      We laughed
in dungeons and scrawled
next week on clover.
But didn't you notice
even then,
how she spawned on us
with her goddamned schemes?
We lounged on sabers
She angled with twaddle.
We rode. She crowded
our rickshaw.
Still we lost her
once when
we caught the train
and left her powdering
her nose. When
I think back on us—
it's a crazy assortment,
roses and dragons.
But
there was space
and Phyllis was there
Phyllis was always there.

For Children

2

A wondrous number is 2.
       There's so much
2 can do!
                     2's less than 3
2's more than 1.
2 is an awful lot of fun!

BILLY

I have a friend named Billy;
Billy's two inches high.
You think this is silly—
so do Billy and I.

Billy lives on my shoulder
underneath my ear.
When Billy starts a singin'
it's awfully hard to hear.

Billy's a million years old;
that's tough to believe, I know
but my proof is irrefutable:
Billy told me so.

Once I lost ol' Billy
when I let my shoulders droop.
But I found him soon again
a swimmin' in the soup.

Billy swings on my hair
and makes it look a wreck
He jumps up on my collar
and scrambles down my neck.

A great little friend is Billy
Even with all his buzzin'.
And if you'd like a pal like him
I'll let you meet his cousin.

THE FROG AND THE DOG

The cat and the rat
were having a spat
on top of an orange tree;

the rat and the cat
stopped the spat.
Now it's quiet, you see.

The cow and the sow
Were having a row
Out behind the canoe;

the sow and the cow
quit the row
and looked for something to do.

The mite and the kite
were having a fight
while flying through the air.

The kite and the mite
finished the fight
and now it's peaceful there.

The frog and the dog
sat on the log
having a wonderful time.

The frog and the dog
jumped off the log
and that's the end of the rhyme.

TWO LITTLE SHOES

Two little shoes
blue little shoes
one fine pair of new little shoes
walking down the street.

Funny shoes
runny shoes
one honey of a pair of shoes
going helter skelter skeet.

Fancy shoes
dancy shoes
prancy shoes
shoes not quite complete.

Two little
blue little
new little shoes
funny
runny
honey shoes
fancy
dancy
prancy shoes
shoes without any feet.

GROWNUP

Lisette
  (age four)
is wearing her mother's gown
  (the white one)
and a fancy green bonnet
  covers her curls.
But the high heels
  (with buckles)
lay discarded beneath a tree—
she walks much better
      in her own shoes.

MUMBLEDEE

There was a yellow fellow named
   bumbledeebee who lived
with his family in a squashy lemon tree.

There was a funny man named
   mumbledee—me who went
out every day on a spree before tea.

Now mumbledee—me
      always grumbled,
"Ah gee, there's nothing much 'round
      for me to see;
I'd like a real jamboree
      on my spree before tea,"
said mumbledee—me.

One day before tea
      he went out for his spree
and stumbled he—
      tumbled, jumbled —
rumbled he
down beneath the lemon tree.
      Beneath the bee tree
fell mumbledee—me.

Now a bee (you'll agree)
(any bee) you see
doesn't like to be
rudely disturbed by a fumbling he,
most especially, most certainly

not beneath his own
squashy tree.
                        So he stung!
OWEEEEEEEE!

OX BOX

A wide and awkward beast the ox is.
He never can be put in boxes.
On my desk stands a dark blue box
absolutely devoid of ox.

In Memory of the Master:
A Tribute to Edgar Lee Masters

SPOON RIVER ANTHOLOGY—1960

Self-portraits in flattering hue
We paint in living days
And place for the world to view
Our mirrors are then hung aside
Distorted oils become the pride
Of those who cannot appraise.
Pictures for studio drawn
Dappled with changing light
Are visions of the dawn
Delusions of the night.

Unchanged within covers rare
Are yet profiles limned of shades
Wastrels, Teachers, Lovers there
Unhoused no more than a picture's fool,
Reflections in an awesome pool
Risen in Stygian glades.
Genius of an artist's eye
Sees midst ambient gloom
To bring forth truth that lies
In the unshadowed tomb.

Spoon River, built upon the lives
Of sleepers on the hill,
Hamlet of the mind survives
For a poet sketched the world he
        saw
Fashion could never bid him draw
His masterpiece living still.
Art is an eternal here

When mirroring the hour
Only truth transcends its year
With all increasing power.

TO EDGAR LEE MASTERS

How can a poet cope with proper?

You had niche, Mr. Masters,
and built a town with wormwood.
Are there Furies
everywhere?
The trick must be knowing
what and when to flee.
Chicago was too narrow
to hold Spoon River.
Did you leave
for dimension or perspective?

Either way, I dedicate
my perplexity to you,
for you would scoff at both
the doubt and dedication
and I agree such things
do not deserve consideration.
Still my dilemma is real—
more real than Chicago,
though not yet as real as your village.

MODERN EPITAPHS
Written after reading
Spoon River Anthology by Edgar Lee Masters

WILLIAM J. JONES, JR.

I arrived this earth, 3 a.m., February 1942
All pertinent details of the birth were printed on a blue
        bordered card
Through infancy and babyhood I held to the course
Delineated by those Dr. draftsmen who chart the progress of Young
        America
At the age of three I entered nursery school
where, according to "Miss Grace," I was cooperative and well
        adjusted
Future reports through the grades continued to be a source of
satisfaction
        to my parents
Other accomplishments included the second base position for the
        Little League
And a First-Class Scout badge earned after three years of steady
        attendance at the Thursday meetings.
They elected me vice-president of the junior class
And my collection of 237 rock 'n' roll records was acknowledged
the
        best in the neighborhood.
My quest for learning finally finished, I stood twenty-fifth in
        Central's
        largest graduating class of 50.
We all got cars for graduation—my crowd
We headed that night for Pete's Place at 70 miles per
I took the wrong turn and went over a cliff.
I shouldn't have left the rest
Dead On Arrival
My tombstone reads,
In Pace Requiescat

MRS. J. CLAYTON VAN SKINE

Ungrateful folk of Twin Forks
You who gathered for my funeral in new black bonnets
Praising my never ceasing devotion to good causes
Which took all my leaving naught for self nor him who bore
   the name of husband.
Not for reward; I was rich
But for community good I strove to rid my town of foreign taints
   and strains
Leading the "Daughters of the Flag"
We tore that scarlet mural from the schoolhouse walls
And from the library's secluded shelves cast out seditious books.
Twas I kept them from laying dark flesh to mingle with this native
   soil
And now the plants above my grave, scarce seen two summers, are
left
   untended.
The Home for Wayward Girls which bore my name has been
removed to the
   city.

Remembrance

AN ENDING

Why do we rend the days with our grief?
He would not have it so
For he respected life
Too much to bewail its passing
And death was too obscure
To have a place in his philosophy.
The thing has been decreed
   (he would have said)
So if you have to pause
Let it be to reason
Not to mutter or complain
Then go on to ponder things
That somehow can be explained.
Death is a void, that's all.
He would not toy with idle questions
For reason was his God and he was twenty-seven.

The hospital halls were narrow and bleak.
Arthur's room was small.
This was all that there was
Of the world where we kept our vigil.
In this swaddled sphere
Of bottled blood and antiseptic dreams
We awaited omens
Although we knew
His body's bane would grow
And only death could free us.
He ate very well today.
The night rest was only fair.

His temperature went down
To one hundred three degrees.
Our hopes could only hang on hours.
Why then lament the ending of this tragic guard?

Do we weep for the wasted figure
That lay upon this bed?
He was but a symbol
Of a once fervent fire. Still
We cherished the fading flame
And lived for Arthur in those mongrel hours.
We kept our watch for life
Because we knew
We could not wait for death
Or we would fail his need.
A hypothesis was stated:
A proposition was created
By the cancer of his flesh:
Given two realities
And a singular existence—
With Arthur we understood, accepted and agreed.

Arthur is dead.
His mother drowns in a vortex of tears,
Her center untimely ripped away.
His wife holds a scratch pad of all their past
    (four years go by so quickly)
And cried for blueprints she will never read.
Fathers, brothers, friends: we all bemoan

The print too soon exposed.
Do we weep for Arthur
Or ourselves and what we know?

The moment is inadequate
To grasp the years.
A life still green
Has been dispersed
Beneath the callous sky.
But those who bear its unripe grain
Must also wither soon.
Why mourn the single seed?
We must mourn
In defiance of a Fate
That chalks our horoscope on clouds
Which pass before the sun.
We sow our grief
Until the storm can break
For Aquarius and Leo must not drown.
Come then, let us reap
In the uplands of rejoicing.
Let us breathe
The seconds scented with the spring.
Bask in tranquil hours
When the turbid time has cleared.
Mourners, seek the gestures
That will sound the slackened string.
Turn our brief music
to Hosanna.

FUNERAL

It is a day like any other
in the spring
when the world has no time
for those who die.
The chapel is filled
With phrases. I hear
the passing generations.

My father's casket is covered
with roses.
What can I do when
the flowers fade?
The rabbi prays
in Hebrew.
I do not understand.

Still I know
the wind has swirled
past this place;
the harvest is apportioned;
the soil is churned.
His grave will be deep.

I shiver now.
It is cold
at the funeral of my father.

MY FATHER DIED

My father died last month
and today I am wondering whether
the trains will travel on time.
He was stiff in his coffin. I touched his hand.
At the market place this morning the melons
Were firm and I bought some for the children.
His grave lies cold in me.
The days are getting longer now.
Yesterday I saw crocuses coming up.

ON THE ANNIVERSARY OF HIS DEATH
for my father

Legless tables,
plates, and golden stains,
cuckoo flying wildly
round the clock,
satined butlers dancing
wine into a pot—
I sit with Father,
cross-legged on the floor,
strangers reflected
in the dishes.

I leave and walk
and walk and watch
women on stoops
disrupting skies,
wingless birds fluttering
where living haunts
those who die.
Lonely as streets
that never end.
I worry back
the way I came.
Flowers pass
beyond me on the lot.

IMMORTAL

I hear
The children calling
As they run across the meadow
Not knowing of shadow worlds
That lie beyond their play.
They throw a ball
Expending all the moment
And judgment is scrawled
With chalk on a broken board.
                    I see
The oarsmen pulling
Proud and strong against the tide
Unmindful of distant shores
That lie beyond the quay.
They do not hear
The cheering boys applaud, nor
See the weary gaze
Of those who have raced before.
                    I pity
The mourner smiling
And unable to believe
In the power of the world
That lies beyond the day.
He sees young men
As they bear the coffin while
Reality passes:
Destiny dwindles to a night.
                        I know that when
The mourner dies

I will weep for him. Will others
Someday stop and mourn for me?
I do not think so—
Death is for the old
And I have always ridden
In racing boats. I am
A child of the meadows.

HE WAS OUR FRIEND

"We have nothing to fear but fear itself" as
        these words rang through the air.
A brand-new era thus began for this country
        so large and fair.
An era of jobs, new hope, new life and money
        for all to spend.
He did this for us: because he was our friend.

Though he was stricken from a dread disease and his
        legs were tired and spent.
With remarkable courage he forged ahead and
        became our president.
To this great country of ours he gave his all until the very end.
He did this for us: because he was our friend.

He did not forget the children with paralysis infantile,
To cure them he worked with his heart and soul so
        that they again could smile.
He started the "March of Dimes" to get funds so
        their twisted limbs could mend.
He did this for us: because he was our friend.

When the dread clouds of battle gathered on a distant
        foreign shore
It was he who warned this country that we had better
        prepare for war.
He built up our Army and Navy and got our planes to land to
        defend.
He did this for us: because he was our friend.

He brought us through days of darkness, with his leadership
    our nation was blessed.
Now on the eve of victory he has been called to his final rest.
The reason why he had to leave us now no one can comprehend.
We only know that we miss him: because he was our friend.

Road to Love

WATERCOLOR II

His mood was soft, soft like unruffled down;
All summer long his dreams would tiptoe round
The corner looking for a water-ice.
A blue sky was filled with pillows,
Big white puffs of cotton billows.
Yet still his drifting life was not disturbed
By cumulous ships on the edge of the world.
He was Aladdin who saw a king's wealth
As it passed by his chair—rare emeralds
And gold borne by pale jinni in starched coats.

His art was soft with passion sometimes sketched
In small concentric spheres of cautious blue.
The canvas will be finished Monday.
No work today for it is Sunday.
So he walked by the ocean watching waves
Till cloud-pent storms ripped forth and reigned
Like Furies on the sea. Then he fled
Back to the easel of his studio room
Where free from the stare of the troubled moon
He drew pictures of the pitching rain.

His love was soft, grown from philosophy.
Thirty is the age to marry.
Pick a wife and do not tarry.
And thus he filled a vacuum with a void.
Now two walked through the calm of muted dusk
Led by vibrations from unplayed lutes;
Then two stopped for rest on the mountainside

And watched a heron flying out of sight;
The bird flew to its roost beyond the mountain
Where twilight burned in crimson on the sky.

His death was soft for it was in April
When the world has no time for those who die.
Over his procession lamb-clouds romped
Unnoticed by the solemn row of black.
The gallery will be closed from two till three
In respect for the artist's memory.
And also in respect his widow wept,
Wept with the emptiness of her despair.
She never knew that her grave tears were shed
For the lost colors of a fading sun.

ON TUESDAY

This morning I walked,
moving awake with the north-flying geese,
believing the just risen sun.
As all my days, this one will be for you.
I collect things to tell you:
an angled shadow
spectacular on the spring sidewalk,
twilight that unfolds and flies,
an existential variance,
or a breeze resonating with the night.
There are friends at corners,
partings that never matter,
afternoon pulled like wire
behind the circled view.
And all the minutes as I wait for Friday
when we will demolish nothing with our smiles.

ALONE

I am badly alone
desiring you.
In a million ways
you move about the room
while night holds my secret.
Once even time could not
ride the spaces of our love.
How memory spreads
knowing forever
the nest of your thighs.

DEMANDS

The flowers pass beyond me
and the harsh bird cries—
I cannot find the tall man
with heart blue eyes.
Night's accents
howl in crevices.
Demands keep breaking in—
morning comes cold
and unresolved.

One year,
one anniversary,
one death—
morning is unresolved.

SEPARATION

Night bends with the weight
  of your parting.
Time is long in the wound
  of the wind.
Bare branches of trees
  rap the window—
Once I watched
  a boy alone
  with his horn,

  pasture grass
  curved down,

  regatta boats
  beyond the turn

and now I plead with these
knowing you will never understand.

AUTUMN REUNION

I plodded thru the summer of your journey, thru
Days gossamered in phantasy of return,
Until the grapevine of affection
Brought word of travel's end
And your presence stirred across my dream-webbed
       world.

Fearing reticence, I besomed the wafting visions
And indifference, jagged against the weavings of a distant
       loom,
I came with hope entwined
To stand unbidden at your door where

In the reality of your gold-graven name
I recognized my moment's vaulting flight,
Then tossed the hollow surety—
A suppliant's right against the greater grant of love.

You opened on my uncertainty
And our vibrations colliding filled
Crevices of neglect becoming
Masters of the reunion.
The September sun now brilliant warmed to summer glow
Our world beneath the drifting autumn mist.

FRUITION

Upward toward sunlight
the tree grew from our hands
shielded by a sheath of love
it breathed beyond demand
until a jealous rain
drenched the lovely roots
then the wounded branches
brought forth a mottled fruit.

I tasted, and I planted
the seeds in deepest woods;
twisted and distended boughs
sprouted where I stood.
Then I saw my lover's eyes
as blooms on this awful tree
and lonely in a vacant head
his heart stared down at me.

ON AN OVERTURNED TREE

We sat and talked
about forever—
that windy day,
the wind's own day,
a grayish speck of time.

How tame the sun looked
all tied back with clouds—
we talked of sapwood
and peeled the bark away.

Then memory rushed by,
on a runaway breeze,
skittish as afternoon.
Ho for that gust
and how we laughed
as it tumbled
thicket high—
a russet leaf
and its windflaw steed
beyond the broken tree.

But laughter subsides on
the wind's kind of day
and memory is stronger
than skies—our talk
turned to blowy things
and ways that a love can die.

www.ingramcontent.com/pod-product-compliance
Lightning Source LLC
LaVergne TN
LVHW051755080426
835511LV00018B/3324